Photo by Martha Swope

A scene from the New York Shakespeare Festival production of "The Swan." Set design by James Youmans.

THE SWAN

BY ELIZABETH EGLOFF

★

★

DRAMATISTS
PLAY SERVICE
INC.

SPECIAL NOTE
Anyone receiving permission to produce THE SWAN is required to give credit to the Author as sole and exclusive Author of the Play on the title page of all programs distributed in connection with performances of the Play and in all instances in which the title of the Play appears for purposes of advertising, publicizing or otherwise exploiting the Play and/or a production thereof. The name of the Author must appear on a separate line, in which no other name appears, immediately beneath the title and in size of type equal to 50% of the size of the largest, most prominent letter used for the title of the Play. No person, firm or entity may receive credit larger or more prominent than that accorded the Author. The following acknowledgments must appear on the title page in all programs distributed in connection with performances of the Play:

Performed at Actors Theatre of Louisville.

Subsequently Produced by La Jolla Playhouse
Des McAnuff, Artistic Director, Terrence Dwyer, Managing Director.

Original New York Production
New York Shakespeare Festival.

SPECIAL NOTE ON SONGS AND RECORDINGS
For performances of copyrighted songs, arrangements or recordings mentioned in this Play, the permission of the copyright owner(s) must be obtained. Other songs, arrangements or recordings may be substituted provided permission from the copyright owner(s) of such songs, arrangements or recordings is obtained; or songs, arrangements or recordings in the public domain may be substituted.

For Patrick

ACKNOWLEDGMENT

Deepest thanks to: Rafeal Clements, Gabrielle Cody, Sean Cullen, Morgan Jenness, Mary Mara, Marcus Stern and James Youmans.

THE SWAN was produced by the La Jolla Playhouse (Des McAnuff, Artistic Director; Terrence Dwyer, Managing Director), in La Jolla, California, on September 8, 1993. It was directed by Lisa Peterson; the set design was by Robert Brill; the costume design was by Janice Benning; the lighting design was by John Martin; the original music and sound design was by John Gromada and the stage manager was Paul Jefferson. The cast was as follows:

DORA .... Susan Berman
KEVIN .... Joseph Urla
SWAN .... Michael Harris

THE SWAN was produced by the Joseph Papp Public Theater (George C. Wolfe, Artistic Director), in New York City, in November, 1993. It was directed by Les Waters; the set design was by James Youmans; the costume design was by David Woolard; the lighting design was by Ken Posner; the original music and sound design was by John Gromada and the stage manager was Buzz Cohen. The cast was as follows:

DORA .... Frances McDormand
KEVIN .... David Chandler
SWAN .... Peter Stormare

THE SWAN was developed with the help of Midwest Playlabs.

CHARACTERS

DORA, a nurse
KEVIN, a milkman
BILL, a swan/man

TIME

The present.

PLACE

Somewhere in Nebraska.

NOTE: "The Name Game" is a rock n' roll song recorded by Shirley Ellis.

THE SWAN

Scene 1

Night. Nebraska. The dingy living-room of a split-level house. A fan rattles, blowing hot air slowly around the room.

There is a sofa-bed, and a kitchen counter. A heavy wooden door leads to a screen-door, which leads to the prairie out back. An enormous plate-glass window reveals a black sky. No stars.

A truck approaches from the distance, its headlights surging through the open door. They fill the room, revealing a woman asleep from exhaustion on the sofa. She is in a white uniform, with white stockings, and white shoes. Her name is Dora.

The headlights subside, and drain out the other side of the house.

Suddenly there is a bump, as something hits the window. A shock reverberates. The big wooden door slams shut.

DORA. Hello? *(She turns in her sleep. Quiet. The phone rings. It rings several times. She can barely pick up the receiver.)* Duane? *(She is sleeping. The receiver falls from her ear. Pause. Somewhere, something cries out: a strangled sort of bark. It cries out over and over, until she finally opens her eyes. She struggles. Sits up. She turns on the light and sees the window. There is an enormous crack spreading over it like a spider, from top to bottom.)* Jesus God. *(Outside, the thing is still barking. She gets a flashlight, and starts for the door. She stops, goes under the bed and gets a rope. An ax. Carries them to*

7

*the screen door, throws it open, and steps into the back yard. From
the back yard, she turns the flashlight on the window. The light skit-
ters across the crack, then turns to the ground where something shrieks.
It looks like an animal. It is arching its neck, throwing its wings up,
everything ruffled. It looks like a radioactive snowflake. It is barking
at her, hysterically. She screams. It screams. She screams.)*

Scene 2

*It becomes dawn. The black sky in the window becomes a col-
orless sky, a colorless plain. A wasteland.*

Dora is asleep in a chair, holding a rifle.

*On the floor is a large laundry basket — in it is an enor-
mous swan.*

*The screen door opens, and a man in white comes in with
two bottles of milk. His name is Kevin. He goes to the refrigerator, and puts them inside. He notices the swan. He goes
to Dora, and taps her shoulder. She wakes.*

KEVIN.   What's that?
DORA.   A swan.
KEVIN.   You're kidding. What's the window?
DORA.   He ran into it. What time is it?
KEVIN.   Six o'clock. You owe me 3 dollars and 80 cents.
DORA.   I don't have any money. *(She goes off. He is staring at
the swan.)*
KEVIN.   You don't have 3 dollars and 80 cents?
DORA'S VOICE.   I HAD THE FUNNIEST DREAM LAST
NIGHT.
KEVIN.   Me, too. I dreamed I gained 200 pounds. Carol kept

telling me to go on a diet. What's happening to you, she said, I don't know you anymore. It was horrible. *(Beat.)* Did you eat, yet? *(He goes to the refrigerator, opens the door, and looks in.)*

DORA'S VOICE. KEVIN, I JUST WOKE UP.

KEVIN. I know. You don't have a thing in here.

DORA'S VOICE. HAVE SOME MILK.

KEVIN. You mind? *(A toilet flushes off-stage. He pours himself a glass of milk, and is finding a box of pizza as Dora reappears, brushing her hair.)*

DORA. I dreamed there was a man sitting on the edge of my sofa. Naked.

KEVIN. Naked?

DORA. It was Duane. And he was chewing on a pack of cigarettes. And I said, Duane, why did you leave me? And he said he didn't leave me, he just went out for a pack of cigarettes, only the drugstore was closed, so he had to go to Paris, and when he got to Paris he'd forgotten his wallet, so he had to call up the President, only the President was dead. Then he took me in his arms and he kissed me, and we got married and moved away and I was so relieved.

KEVIN. Relieved?

DORA. Like there was an enormous weight off my shoulders.

KEVIN. And I suppose I'm the enormous weight.

DORA. Kevin. *(She is taking off her white dress, and stepping into another exactly like it.)*

KEVIN. What's that?

DORA. What?

KEVIN. That. *(Nodding to the uniform.)* You going to work?

DORA. Yes.

KEVIN. You were going to quit.

DORA. They canceled the staff meeting.

KEVIN. You don't have to explain.

DORA. They did.

KEVIN. I love you.

DORA. I love you too.

KEVIN. I want you to quit.

DORA. You can barely support Carol.

KEVIN. Carol doesn't mind.

9

DORA. How are you going to support Carol and me? You can't.

KEVIN. I can.

DORA. Do me. *(He struggles with the zipper on the back of her dress.)*

KEVIN. You don't want me to support you. You say you do, but you don't. You never did.

DORA. Oh now. *(The zipper goes up. He finishes his milk, and steps on a spider.)*

KEVIN. You've got spiders all over the place.

DORA. Spiders are lucky. *(She shakes a spider out of her shoe. He is tearing off another slice of pizza.)*

KEVIN. If you were unhappy about something, if something about us was making you unhappy, Dora ...

DORA. Yes?

KEVIN. You'd tell me, wouldn't you? You'd say it?

DORA. Of course.

KEVIN. Kiss me. *(They kiss.)* I just want you to be happy, Dora. Stay home. Relax. Have fun. Clean the house once in a while. This would be a beautiful house if only you'd clean it. *(She picks up her nursing cap, puts it on her head.)*

DORA. I know. *(She picks up her purse and sweater. Goes to the door, opens it.)*

KEVIN. I'm going to get you another window. Get you a nice double-pane. Easy to clean.

DORA. That will be nice.

KEVIN. The swan's dead.

DORA. The swan is not dead.

KEVIN. He's in a coma.

DORA. He's sleeping.

KEVIN. He's unconscious.

DORA. Stop it.

KEVIN. Something's wrong with him. Really.

DORA. Kevin. Take the pizza outside. NOW, KEVIN! *(As he tears off another slice of pizza.)* How many is that?

KEVIN. WHAT DO YOU CARE? *(He goes out. She follows.)*

10

Scene 3

The sun shifts to the other side of the house, sending shadows across the floor. The swan darkens.

Somewhere, a car door slams. Dora enters, and throws her purse on the sofa-bed. She goes to the swan and stands, looking down at it. Cautiously, she leans a little closer. A little closer.

Suddenly the phone rings. She picks it up.

DORA. *(Into the phone.)*
Hi, Lillian. Did you get my message? No, this is not a duck. This is a swan, I was all set to hit it with the ax. Call me back. *(She hangs up, and dials. She unpins her cap. Into the phone.)*

I'd like to leave a message for Dr. Crawley, please. That's D-O-R-A Dora, Hand H-A-N-D. I'm the lady with the swan. Yes, and I'm a little concerned. Thank you. *(She hangs up. She sits down and starts taking off her shoes. The phone rings again. She picks it up. Into the phone.)*

Hello? Because I can't. Because I'm waiting for the doctor, that's why. It certainly did. Right into the window. I want somebody to pay for it. Kevin is going to pay for it. I called the insurance. *(She spots something crawling across the floor. She hits it with her shoe. The swan shudders, and seems to grow a little larger.)*

You should come out and see it, Lillian, you really should. You've never seen a swan this big. This swan is so big, it's the size of the house. Which one? Him? Forget it. *(An arm is reaching out from under the swan's wing, and exploring the floor. It finds support and begins to push. And now, another arm. Dora is watching something crawl across the back of her sofa.)*

Lillian, you tell that man to pay you back your ten thousand dollars, THEN you'll think about marrying him. I never heard of such a thing. Take the money, Lillian. Not the man, the money. Take the MONEY. *(Dora looks up as the wings, feath-*

11

ers, skin, everything falls back, and a man rolls out of the basket, skit-
ters, and stands up on his feet, new-born. Beat. Into the phone.)
    Lillian, I'll call you back. *(She hangs up. For a moment, they*
stare at each other. Suddenly, he barks at her. Dora yelps, jumps off
the bed, grabs a kitchen chair in self-defense. He bangs his way around
the living-room, searching for air, falling, barking, getting up again,
turning over the furniture. Dora finds the gun and trains it on him.)
    Hold it! I said HOLD IT! I SAID, STOP RIGHT THERE!
(He topples toward a glass lamp. She grabs it before it hits the floor.
Suddenly he turns, sees the window, and runs head-on into it. The
cold feel of glass on his skin stops him, dead. He is glued to the glass.
Everything stops. The telephone is ringing. Dora puts down the lamp
and grabs it. Into the phone.)
    Hello? *(The swan is touching every part of his body to the glass.*
Into the phone.)
    Lillian, I can't talk right now. I'll call you back. *(She hangs*
up. He is exploring the cracks in the window with his fingers. She
trains the gun on him, and takes a step toward him.) Get away from
there! Shoo! Shoo! SHOO! *(The phone rings. She picks it up. Into*
the phone.)
    Lillian, I said I'm busy. I'll get back to you as soon as I
can. *(She goes to the screen door, and props it open with a chair.*
Then she grabs a kitchen towel, and tries to flick him out of the house,
like a fly.)
    GO ON. Go on, now. Get. *(She flicks him lightly with the*
towel. He turns, angrily.)
    That's all right. You get along, now. You get out of here.
(She flicks him again. He turns on her with a hiss and a bark.)
    Hey! HEY! Don't you—get away! Get away, now! *(He keeps*
coming. She throws a chair in his way. He trips over it, keeps com-
ing. Finally, she opens the refrigerator and throws a box of pizza at
him. He starts to devour the box, and is discovering the pizza inside,
when a truck pulls up outside, honks.)
    Holy Moses! It's Kevin! HIDE! *(She slams the door. He stares*
as she runs around the house, pulling the shades and trying to whoosh
him into the bedroom.)
    Go on! In! IN! IN! *(She throws the pizza into the bedroom. He*
goes after it. Kevin is at the screen door. He tries it, but it doesn't

open. He raps on it.)
KEVIN'S VOICE.   DORA? DORA, HONEY? YOU IN THERE?
(She freezes. Kevin moves to the window. He is trying to peer inside.
The swan appears at the door of the bedroom, curious.) DORA, IT'S
KEVIN! YOU ALL RIGHT?
DORA.   *(To the swan.)* Go on! Go on! Go!
KEVIN'S VOICE.   DORA? SOMETHING WRONG?
DORA.   Nothing, Kevin! *(She runs into the bedroom, and returns*
a moment later with a bathrobe, and tries to stuff the swan into it.)
KEVIN'S VOICE.   WHAT'S GOING ON IN THERE? DORA,
YOU ALL RIGHT? DORA, SPEAK TO ME?
DORA.   I'll be right there! *(To the swan.)* Put this on.
KEVIN'S VOICE.   I'M COMING IN, DORA! I'M COMING IN
RIGHT NOW!
DORA.   Kevin, don't! Kevin, for God's sake, Kevin!
KEVIN'S VOICE.   STAND BACK, DORA!
DORA.   Kevin, NO! *(There is a gunshot, and the door swings open.*
Kevin stands there, the gun in one hand, a bottle of milk in the other.)
Oh, Kevin. *(He takes a step inside the room, sets down the bottle,*
and waves the smoke away with one hand.)
KEVIN.   Dora? You all right?
DORA.   I'm fine.
KEVIN.   You okay?
DORA.   I'm fine.
KEVIN.   Then why did you make me shoot off the lock?
DORA.   I didn't tell you to —
KEVIN.   Goddamn, Dora. I could have got hurt.
DORA.   I didn't tell you to shoot off the lock. *(He sees the*
swan.)
KEVIN.   Who's he?
DORA.   Nobody. He's a, Kevin, put the — Kevin, put the gun
down — *(To the swan.)* Hey! Get out of there! Get away! *(The*
swan is trying to take hold of the gun. Dora pushes the swan away.)
Kevin, this is not what you think it is. Are you listening?
KEVIN.   I'm listening. *(She is tying the belt of the bathrobe around*
the swan.)
DORA.   He's a, he's a swan, Kevin. He's the swan.
KEVIN.   He is?

13

DORA. The swan. He's the swan.

KEVIN. He's a man.

DORA. That, too.

KEVIN. Dora.

DORA. Anyway, I came home and I could see he was running a little fever so I called Dr. Crawley.

KEVIN. Dr. Crawley?

DORA. Dr. Crawley is a perfectly good doctor.

KEVIN. Go on.

DORA. So then I called Lillian, and I'm in the middle of talking to Lillian, and he changes into, well, he changes into THIS.

KEVIN. I see.

DORA. I know it sounds crazy, but there it is. *(She throws the swan the rest of the pizza.)*

KEVIN. What did you do that for?

DORA. Kevin, it's been in the fridge for 3 days.

KEVIN. Well, shoot. That was a perfectly good pizza.

DORA. Put the gun down. *(As he puts the gun back in its holster.)*

KEVIN. You don't love me.

DORA. Kevin, do you think I'd have let you in, if it was what you think it was?

KEVIN. You didn't let me in. I had to shoot the door off.

DORA. Yes, thank you very much. Now who's going to fix it?

KEVIN. Why didn't you open it?

DORA. Are you going to fix it?

KEVIN. Why didn't you open it?

DORA. I'm not going to fix it.

KEVIN. Okay, fine.

DORA. I don't know how to fix it.

KEVIN. I said, FINE. I'll get somebody from town to fix it. *(The phone rings. Dora picks it up.)*

DORA. Lillian, I'm in the middle of a discussion. I'll speak to you when I'm able. *(As she hangs up, the swan suddenly chokes on the pizza. Dora goes to it, and slaps it on the back. It coughs. She gets it a bowl of milk, and sets it on the floor. The swan slurps from*

14

it, then rolls over with a crash, and is instantly asleep. Pause.)
KEVIN.   I think you should call another doctor.
DORA.   I called Dr. Crawley.
KEVIN.   Not Dr. Crawley. An animal doctor. I want you to call the vet.
DORA.   Okay.
KEVIN.   I'm telling you, Dora, if this is a swan, it belongs in the zoo, the hospital, wherever. It does not belong in the same house where you live. It's not healthy. It's not even sanitary.
DORA.   You're right. You're absolutely right. You're right.
KEVIN.   Are you going to call?
DORA.   I certainly am.
KEVIN.   Where are you going?
DORA.   I'm going to change.
KEVIN.   You don't love me.
DORA.   Yes I do.
KEVIN.   No you don't. If you did, you wouldn't do this to me. DORA? *(She is gone. He exits after her.)*

Scene 4

The sun sinks into the floor. Night.

A light comes on in the bathroom.

Dora enters in her slip. The swan is still lying on the floor. He is weeping in his sleep.

She lies down on the sofa, pulls the blanket over herself, and closes her eyes.

The swan is still weeping. She puts the pillow over her head. He's still weeping. Finally, she gets up. She brings her pillow over to the swan, and cautiously slips it under his head. He's

15

still weeping. She gets her blanket and carefully drops it over his body. He stops weeping. Silence.

She sits down on the sofa, and watches him sleep.

Scene 5

Late afternoon. Kevin is outside on a ladder, taping the window in a big X.

Dora is inside, talking to him through the broken window.

The swan is still lying on the living room floor. His eyes are open, and he is staring into space.

DORA.   I told them, "You can put that man in physical therapy or occupational therapy, but you're not taking him out of here." Because he's mine. Because it's my floor, I have a relationship with that man, I'm the only one who knows how to take care of him, and because you know what, Kevin? The man has no arms and no legs. No arms and no legs. Not even a little STUB. *(A jumbo jet is approaching. Kevin says something.)* What? *(Kevin says it again.)* I can't hear you. *(As the sound of the jet recedes.)*
KEVIN.   TAPE. WE NEED MORE TAPE. *(Dora crosses to the kitchen, and opens a drawer, and finds some tape. She is standing there, watching the swan, when Kevin appears next to her. He takes the tape out of her hand.)* What are you doing?
DORA.   He's not moving.
KEVIN.   Well you wouldn't take my advice.
DORA.   He just lies there and cries. *(Kevin goes out. She stands there for a moment, watching the swan. She picks up the boom box. She picks a cassette, sticks it in the boom box, and hits Play. It's "The*

16

*Name Game."** She looks at the swan. No response. She crosses back to the window, as Kevin reappears and starts up the ladder. Suddenly they both turn. The swan is sitting up. He is looking at the boom-box. He climbs to his feet, and goes to the boom-box. He circles around it, and finally, with one long arm, reaches out and grabs it. He carries it to the sofa, where he lies down with it, holding it in his arms like a lover.)*

Scene 6

*Another day. The swan is lying on the sofa in cut-offs, listening to a song such as "The Name Game"** on the boom-box, playing with the volume.*

There are orange peels scattered over the sofa, and pizza crusts all over the floor. Kevin enters from the bedroom, carrying a vacuum cleaner.

KEVIN. TURN THAT THING DOWN. *(The swan looks at him, and turns the music up. Kevin puts down the vacuum and goes around the room, stooping and picking up orange peels and pizza crusts. Finally he straightens.)* I SAID — HEY! Turn that — turn that — *(As Kevin approaches the boom box, the swan barks at him.)* Goddamit. TURN IT DOWN. *(He goes to the boom box, and turns it off. The swan barks at him again. Kevin picks up the vacuum cleaner, and approaches the sofa.)* Get off the sofa. GET OFF THE SOFA. *(The swan turns the boom box on again.)* ALL RIGHT KIDDO. I'VE HAD IT. I'VE HAD IT. *(He turns on the vacuum cleaner, and starts sucking at the swan, who backs off, hissing. The encounter is about to get ugly, when Dora kicks open the screen door.)*

* See Special Note on Songs and Recordings on copyright page.

She is in her uniform, and carrying a bag of groceries. Kevin instantly lowers the vacuum.)

DORA.   Hi, honey!

KEVIN.   Hi. *(As Dora sets the groceries on the counter, Kevin turns off the music savagely. The bird hisses. Kevin threatens him. The bird hushes.)*

DORA.   Have a nice day? *(She starts to unpack the groceries.)*

KEVIN.   Okay. You?

DORA.   Mr. Pfizer had his brain surgery.

KEVIN.   Mind if we talk?

DORA.   I've got groceries.

KEVIN.   He got into the front yard today. He was going through Mrs. Middle's garbage.

DORA.   Oh God.

KEVIN.   Mrs. Middle was in the back yard. It was this close, Dora. This close.

DORA.   I'll talk to him.

KEVIN.   Don't talk to him. Get rid of him. IT. *(Dora looks at the swan, whose ear is glued to the silent radio.)*

DORA.   I can't do that.

KEVIN.   DORA! *(As she heads back to the groceries, he grabs her arm, and takes her aside.)* The laundry. The radio. Pizza-boxes. Soda-cans. Look at these orange peels.

DORA.   You've done a wonderful job cleaning up.

KEVIN.   I'm not your slave, Dora. *(She looks at him a moment. Then.)*

DORA.   All right. *(She returns to unpacking groceries. He follows her.)*

KEVIN.   What does that mean all right?

DORA.   It means all right. I heard you. What you said has been heard.

KEVIN.   What are you going to do? *(She hands him a head of lettuce.)*

DORA.   Did you give him the algae? *(He unwraps the lettuce, and starts shredding it into the dog bowl.)*

KEVIN.   Fine, Dora. If you want it that way, I have to tell you. I made an appointment with George Cover.

DORA.   Fine.

KEVIN. We've got to talk to somebody. I can't go on like this. I'm afraid of what will happen to me.

DORA. Nothing's going to happen to you.

KEVIN. Dora, you've got a MAN in your house! *(She hands him a box of sprouts.)* What's this?

DORA. Sprouts.

KEVIN. I know it's sprouts, where did you get them?

DORA. Mrs. Brezinski said he'd like them.

KEVIN. You told Mrs. Brezinski about him?

DORA. Of course. And you know, Kevin — she's a wonderful woman, Kevin. She's going to compile a bibliography on the vertebrate problems of the cygnus buccinator. That's a Trumpeter.

KEVIN. He's not a Trumpeter, Dora.

DORA. Oh yes, he is. You can tell by the length of his neck.

KEVIN. I SAID HE'S NOT A TRUMPETER! *(Silence.)*

DORA. All right, Kevin. What is it? It's not the swan. Is it Carol? I could see why she'd be upset. She's your wife, and here you are, working your poor little fingers to the bone. *(She kisses his fingers.)*

KEVIN. It's not Carol.

DORA. Oh, now. Look at Bill.

KEVIN. ... Bill? *(They turn and look at the bird, who is chewing on the radio.)*

DORA. *(Fondly.)* Isn't he pathetic?

KEVIN. That does it.

DORA. I'm not going to keep him around forever. Just until he gets better, and then I'll let him go.

KEVIN. He's better NOW.

DORA. I don't know. I saw him this morning out back, and he was doing that circle-thing again. I wish he'd stop. It just makes him dizzy.

KEVIN. Dora, I'm calling your bluff. You hear me? I'm calling your bluff. George Cover is expecting us tomorrow morning, are you listening?

DORA. Of course I'm listening.

KEVIN. Tomorrow morning, Dora. 5:30.

DORA. I heard you.

KEVIN. I'm paying for it. 65 dollars.

DORA. Thank you, Kevin.

KEVIN. You'll come?

DORA. Of course I'll come. I've always said we should see a marriage counselor.

KEVIN. Right. *(Dora sets the dog bowl on the floor, and calls to the swan.)*

DORA. Dinner.

KEVIN. I'm going.

DORA. That's a good idea. As for me, I'm going to take a hot bath, shave my legs, and give myself a nice, long pedicure.

KEVIN. That's fine. That's a good idea. Carol wants me to pick up the choir robes.

DORA. Then you'd better hurry.

KEVIN. Right.

DORA. Drive safe.

KEVIN. I'll honk at 5.

DORA. I'll be ready.

KEVIN. It will be good for us, you know. Give us a chance to really get to know each other.

DORA. I can't wait.

KEVIN. Neither can I.

DORA. I love you. *(They kiss. Kevin goes. Dora goes off. After a moment, the sound of the bath water, running. The swan sits alone with his dinner — eating, thinking, and eating. Outside, the sound of birds, twittering. The swan is experimenting with his food, when the birds suddenly explode into flight. He jumps to his feet, runs to the window, and throws himself against the glass. They fly away without him, their shadows pressing over the house until they are gone.)*

Scene 7

Night. Dora and the swan are sitting at the kitchen table, in the middle of a game of checkers. They are staring at the board intently.

DORA.   Strategy. Everything's strategy. You've got to think, and figure out what the other fellow's doing, and then make your move based on strategy. *(She cracks a beer, and reaches for a bag of chips.)*

Of course, the problem is that the other fellow's probably got a strategy, too. And if your strategy doesn't match his strategy, what are you going to do? How are you going to plan? How are you going to think? Answer? You're not. In this case, it will be easier if you try not to plan at all. Try this. Try to block everything out of your mind. Just think of your mind like it's a blank slate. *(She struggles with the bag of chips, and finally opens it with her teeth.)*

It's not easy, is it? And you know what? You're going to hear stories around town about me and my last husband. Don't even think about them. It won't help. You've got to jump. *(She points to the board.)*

Jump. It's the rules. *(He stares at her. She picks up his checker and jumps it over one of her own. Hands her checker to him. He bites it. She takes it out of his mouth.)*

Don't do that. You'll ruin your little teeth. Have a chip. *(She hands him a chip. He takes the whole bag from her, and starts eating them hungrily.)*

Now it's MY turn. *(She jumps 5 times over his checkers, and stacks them on her side of the table. He watches her, icily. She pauses.)*

You've loved somebody, haven't you? I can tell. I can look into your face — in this case, a bird face — and I can see. That's something we've got in common. I've loved somebody, too. Several of them. I loved Franklin and he divorced me. I loved Gerry and he shot himself. I loved Duane and he ran off. Move. *(Pause.)*

Now, of course, I've got Kevin. That great, big debacle of a man. Your move. *(She leans over the board, sets her finger on one of his checkers, and is sliding it into a nearby space, when.)*
SWAN. You don't love me. *(Pause.)*
DORA. Excuse me?
SWAN. If you did, you wouldn't do this to me. *(Another pause.)*
DORA. You can talk. Bill, you can talk. *(She takes a chip out of the bag, and offers it to him.)* Say chip. Chip. Say please can I have a potato chip? *(She holds it out to him. He starts to take it. She pulls it away.)*
SWAN. Please can I have one of those things?
DORA. What?
SWAN. Those.
DORA. Beer? You want a beer?
SWAN. Please could I have a Beer? You want a beer? *(He grabs the chip from her, and she jerks backward, turning her chair over.)*
DORA. Good. Very good. You want it in a glass? *(She stumbles to the refrigerator, gets a beer, and gets a glass. He follows, rattling at her.)*
SWAN. Then why did you make me shoot off the lock?
DORA. Excuse me?
SWAN. *(Overriding.)* Goddamn, Dora. I could have got hurt.
DORA. Sure, Bill. That's it. That's it. That's good. *(She stops. He is biting her hair. He continues to bite her hair for a moment, ruminating. When she speaks, he echoes her.)*
DORA/SWAN. I'll get you a glass. Sit down. Sit. *(She goes to the table, showing him.)* Sit. Stay. That's a good boy. Good boy. I'm going to get you a beer. *(She gets up, and he gets up.)* I said don't get up. Stay there. *(She sits down. He sits down. As she gets up, he gets up. He races her to the refrigerator.)*
I said DON'T COME ANY CLOSER. *(She throws a beer into his hand. He licks the side of it, then takes a long sip. He picks up the bottle from the counter, and takes a long sip of that, too. Finally he stops and looks at her.)*
DORA. What's the matter? *(He twitches — then sinks to the floor, the beers balanced in his hands like two flowers. From his knees, he speaks.)*

SWAN.   Dora Bora Bo Bora. Dora.*
DORA.   Bill? Are you okay? *(He lays his head on her foot, tired.)*
SWAN.   I'm so depressed.
DORA.   Sleep. Sleep. *(She starts to remove her foot. Suddenly he hisses, arching his back horribly, a monster, grabbing her hands. Slowly he pulls her down to the floor, then sets his head on her foot. The hissing dies. He is asleep.)*

Scene 8

Night. Dora is sleeping on the floor, with the swan's head on her foot.

Outside, a breeze is blowing. The swan opens his eyes. The screen door is gently banging against the frame.

He gets up, and goes out.

Scene 9

Early morning. Dora is sleeping on the floor. The swan is sleeping on top of the refrigerator. The wooden door is shut.

A truck pulls into the driveway. There is a honk. The swan raises his head, looks around. Dora sleeps on.

Kevin comes to the door. He tries it. It's locked.

* If "The Name Game" is not used, then a line must be substituted here, rhyming the line of the song with Dora's name.

KEVIN'S VOICE. DORA? IT'S 5:15. OPEN THE DOOR. *(He tries the door again, gives up, and goes to the window. The swan scampers to the window, and positions himself above it. Kevin knocks on the window.)*

IT'S 5:15, DORA. WE'RE DUE AT DOCTOR COVER'S IN 15 — *(He is interrupted by the swan, who jumps down with a horrible hiss and a bark.)*

BILL. HEY, BILL. OPEN THE DOOR. OPEN THE DOOR, BILL ... DORA. *(Kevin comes back to the door. The swan scampers back to it.)*

GOOD BOY. GOOD BOY, BILL. NOW OPEN THE DOOR. OPEN THE DOOR. *(Kevin rattles the doorknob. This time, the swan hisses, raises his wings at him.)*

OKAY, DORA!! IT'S 5:15! NOW WAKE UP!! WAKE UP, DORA!! *(Dora opens her eyes.)*

DORA. Kevin?

KEVIN'S VOICE. OPEN THE DOOR, DORA?- NOW! NOW! NOW! NOW!

DORA. Kevin, what's wrong? *(She goes to the door, and pulls it open.)* It was open.

KEVIN. It was not open. I don't want to make a big thing of it, but it was not open. Get him away from me.

DORA. Bill, get away from him. *(The swan goes under the sofa.)*

KEVIN. He's dangerous.

DORA. Bill can talk.

KEVIN. Get dressed. We've got 15 minutes.

DORA. Bill can talk. *(He goes off.)*

KEVIN'S VOICE. COMB YOUR HAIR.

DORA. Kevin. I'm talking to you. Kevin. *(Kevin returns. He stands in the doorway, holding another white dress.)*

KEVIN. What?

DORA. He talks. He talked to me. Last night. Bill, talk for Kevin. Bill. *(The swan comes out from under the sofa, crosses the room, and tries to climb into the kitchen cabinet.)* Bill. Bill, get out of there. You're going to get footprints all over the pots and pans.

KEVIN. What did he say?

DORA. A lot. *(Now the swan is on top of the refrigerator.)*

KEVIN.　Get down from there.

DORA.　Leave him alone. He's out of the way. Bill? Aren't you going to talk for Kevin? *(They watch the swan settle itself.)* Fine. If that's the way you want it. *(She takes her uniform from Kevin, and goes off.)*

KEVIN.　I saw Dr. Sparring just now.

DORA'S VOICE.　YECCH.

KEVIN.　He wants to know why you've been missing work.

DORA'S VOICE.　I HAVEN'T BEEN MISSING WORK.

KEVIN.　You weren't at work Friday.

DORA'S VOICE.　OH.

KEVIN.　You weren't at work Saturday.

DORA'S VOICE.　I KNOW.

KEVIN.　You were 4 hours late on Sunday.

DORA'S VOICE.　OKAY, OKAY.

KEVIN.　Why won't you quit? You won't quit work, and you won't go to work, either.

DORA'S VOICE.　KEVIN, I'M SORRY, BUT I'VE HAD MORE IMPORTANT THINGS TO DO. *(Dora reappears, pulling her dress down around her hips.)*

KEVIN.　Such as?

DORA.　The library, and Mrs. Brezinski. And then I had to get groceries. You can't buy algae at the IGA, you have to go to a pet store. And you can't buy any pet powder, it has to be a special kind of pet powder. Because the spiders. You know, I think these spiders are coming from BILL. *(She swipes a spider off the wall.)*

KEVIN.　Oh Dora.

DORA.　What does that mean? Oh Dora?

KEVIN.　Never mind.

DORA.　I don't have time for this, Kevin. I'm a busy person. I have a job. I have a house. I have you. I have Bill. These are all major responsibilities. So you know what I'm going to do?

KEVIN.　What?

DORA.　Where are my shoes?

KEVIN.　What are you going to do, Dora?

DORA.　I'm going to quit work.

KEVIN.　... You are? Really?

DORA.　Of course, it will be a financial burden on you, but that's all right, you can handle it.

KEVIN.　Oh God Dora. *(She embraces him.)*

DORA.　This way I can devote myself entirely to Bill, and getting him well and happy. Because when Bill is happy, we'll ALL be happy, won't we?

KEVIN.　Bill?

SWAN.　*(Simultaneously.)* Dora. *(Pause. They turn, and look up at the swan.)*

DORA.　There. He did it. He did it. Bill, do it again. Say something. *(Pause. Nothing. After several moments, the swan turns away, and starts chewing on his skin.)*

KEVIN.　Did he say something?

DORA.　He certainly did. He said my name. Didn't you hear him? Say it, Bill. *(Pause. The swan swings down from the refrigerator, and slides off to the bathroom.)* He's shy. Aren't you, Bill? You're shy. God help me, what did I do with my shoes.... Would you look in the sofa? Kevin? Kevin.

KEVIN.　Excuse me?

DORA.　Forget it. *(She goes off. Kevin goes into the sofa.)*

KEVIN.　My God, don't I have any pride left? What's happened to my sense of dignity?

DORA'S VOICE.　CHEER UP, BILL. I'LL BE HOME IN A COUPLE HOURS, WE'LL DO THE DISHES, WATCH TV.

KEVIN.　Dora.

DORA'S VOICE.　WE'LL CLEAN UP THE HOUSE AND PLANT A GARDEN AND WHEN WE'VE PLANTED A GARDEN MAYBE WE'LL SEE ABOUT BUYING A *POOL.*

KEVIN.　Dora. *(She reappears, putting on her cap.)*

DORA.　Or not. We don't have to buy a pool. We could use Mrs. Brezinski's.

KEVIN.　Dora?

DORA.　What? *(They both bend over the sofa, looking into it.)*

KEVIN.　What's this rabbit doing in the sofa? *(He reaches into the sofa, and picks up a broken rabbit by the ears. It is raw, mangled, and dripping blood.)*

Scene 10

Afternoon. The rain has stopped. The boombox is singing to itself, quietly. The swan enters from the bedroom, wearing a pair of beat-up jeans that are several sizes too large. He is examining himself curiously in a tiny make-up mirror. Dora follows him, shaking the dust out of a beat-up cowboy jacket.

DORA. Duane had a bow and arrow. Duane always used to say, he used to say, Dora Don't Kill Anything Unless You're Planning to Eat It or Wear It. Duane wore more animals than anyone I ever knew. He had crocodile shoes, a cobra belt, a South American buffalo jacket, and a red fox hat. The first time he took me hunting, he caught 16 squirrels and 2 deer. *(She stops, and looks at him.)* That looks much nicer. You need a tie. That one. On the floor.

SWAN. Tie. *(He picks up a bolo tie. She takes it from him, and starts to loop it around his neck.)*

DORA. You ever been married, Bill?

SWAN. Why?

DORA. I am a great supporter of marriage. I don't think people are meant to be alone. I don't think *I* am. Strange things happen to me when I'm alone. Dangerous things.

SWAN. Why?

DORA. Like once I was in bed, smoking a cigarette. And I look up, and there's this man standing in the door. He walked into my house. He just opened the door and walked right into my house.... And he's covered with leaves and there's grass in his hair and mud on his shoes. And he looks so sad and he looks so much like Gerry only that was before I'd ever met Gerry so how could he BUT there's something about him there's something in him that's warm that's alive that's still beating and God! I'm looking at this stranger, I'm looking at this total and complete stranger and I'm thinking Yes you're right love is the only thing that matters if only I could get me some I could laugh again I could eat again I could belong to the world again, and just as I'm about to say Yes, you're him, You're It, You're the One — my cigarette is burning my fingers, I turn to put it out, and by the time I look back, he's gone. Disappeared. Evanesced.

SWAN. Evanesced.

DORA. I never saw him again.

SWAN. Evanesced.

DORA. It's always the way, isn't it? Some people say I shouldn't marry so many, but I have to. They keep disappearing on me. Turn around. *(She throws herself into a chair, as he turns around.)* Not so fast. *(He turns more slowly.)* Now, that's nice. You could wear that sometime when we go out to eat. *(He stops turning. He has noticed her feet. He approaches them, sinks down beside them, and is examining them closely.)*

SWAN. You have nice feet.

DORA. Thank you.

SWAN. ... You have nice ankles.

DORA. Thank you.

SWAN. ... You have nice legs.

DORA. Thank you. *(Suddenly the swan's attention is drawn to a spider crawling across the floor. He dives for it and is eating it, as Kevin appears.)* Why, Kevin. Hello.

KEVIN. Hello yourself. Mrs. Middle is out there.

DORA. What's she doing?

KEVIN. She's watering your flowers.

DORA. It's been raining.

KEVIN. She's concerned. She says you have a man in your house.

DORA. Oh for goodness sake. Bill, put your socks on. Under the shirts. Shirts. *(She points to the shirts, and the swan goes to them.)*

KEVIN. I suppose you're proud of yourself. Mrs. Bukharin was in tears. She was crying, Dora. Crying.

DORA. Did you give her the rabbit?

KEVIN. She doesn't want another rabbit. She wants Bumper.

DORA. I'm sorry.

KEVIN. Yes, well. She threw herself into my arms. Do you know what that means? A woman of her stature, a woman of her reputation? Mrs. Bukharin threw herself into my arms and wept. *(The swan is watching them.)*

DORA.   Bill. Why don't you go take a bath? You'd like that. Go sit in the bath and we can look at socks later. Go on. *(Bill drops the socks, and shuffles off to the bathroom.)*

KEVIN.   Nice jacket.

DORA.   It belonged to Gerry.

KEVIN.   Sort of morbid, don't you think?

DORA.   Gerry's dead. Bill is alive. *(Kevin goes over to the boombox, and turns it off.)*

KEVIN.   Where were you, Dora?

DORA.   Where was I when?

KEVIN.   This morning. 5:30. The third morning in a row.

DORA.   I took Bill out to Red Lake. We saw the sunrise.

KEVIN.   In the rain?

DORA.   You weren't here, or I would have invited you.

KEVIN.   Dora, I don't have a lot of time. I expected you at Doctor Cover's. We both expected you. We waited 15 minutes for you, and then I had to reschedule.

DORA.   Thank you, Kevin.

KEVIN.   Tomorrow at the same time. *(Beat.)* I don't mean to be short with you, Dora.

DORA.   I know you don't.

KEVIN.   You have to pay for the appointment, you know, whether you make it or not.

DORA.   Well, that's silly.

KEVIN.   It is not silly. It's professional. That's what professionals do.

DORA.   I'm paying you back. I am. I'm keeping track of every penny I owe you.

KEVIN.   You said you wouldn't take him out of the house. That's what you said. You promised.

DORA.   It was dark out.

KEVIN.   You promised.

DORA.   I didn't promise. I would never promise a thing like that.

KEVIN.   What if you'd gotten caught? What if somebody saw you? The police? The neighbors? Hell, the neighbors HAVE seen you.

DORA.   They haven't seen us.

KEVIN.   Mrs. Middle? Mrs. Bukharin?

DORA.   Not Mrs. Bukharin.

KEVIN.   You don't think they talk to each other? You think nobody in this town talks to each other? They're my customers. You think my customers don't talk to each other?

DORA.   Kevin, don't be mad. Kevin. Kevin, come on. Give us a little kiss.

KEVIN.   What are you, crazy?

DORA.   Just a kiss. Just a little kiss. Just an eentsy-weentsy little kiss.

KEVIN.   Dora, you seem to be completely unaware of the problem.

DORA.   I'm not unaware of the problem, and you don't have to yell at me.

KEVIN.   I'm not yelling.

DORA.   You're getting very loud.

KEVIN.   I'm not yelling. I'm talking to you rationally like a human being. I'm trying to have some kind of EXCHANGE HERE. *(Suddenly the swan bursts through the front door into the room. He has mud on his knees, and mud on his hands. He is carrying something in his mouth, and drops it in front of Dora. She screams.)* It's a mouse.

DORA.   It's dead.

SWAN.   Mmmiles Out Up Up I hmmmmm bead sssspotted you Tree Bird Goddess tie tying sheets to a snake Clothes Clothesline Your eye hmmmm Your eye hmmmm Your eye like a fire, your lips hmmmmmm BUG Red apple Darling! Ah darling! If I was your lover I would surround you and take you prisoner, I would lay siege to your doorstep, I would swallow you whole like a stone. *(Kevin and Dora stare at him. Blackout.)*

Scene 11

A crash of thunder. Night. Rain. The house is dark. The swan is sitting in the window, wearing a dirty old trench coat, listening to a song such as "The Name Game,"* and watching the storm pass overhead.

Outside, the sound of Kevin's truck, pulling up. Two doors slam. Dora and Kevin's voices, fighting.

KEVIN'S VOICE. IT'S PSYCHOLOGY.
DORA'S VOICE. THIS IS NOT PSYCHOLOGY.
KEVIN'S VOICE. HE'S A PSYCHIATRIST.
DORA'S VOICE. HE'S NOT A PSYCHIATRIST.
KEVIN'S VOICE. GIVE ME THE KEY.
DORA'S VOICE. NO.
KEVIN'S VOICE. GIVE ME THE KEY.
DORA'S VOICE. NO.
KEVIN'S VOICE. I SAID GIVE ME THE KEY.
DORA'S VOICE. YOU'RE NOT ALLOWED TO COME IN MY HOUSE.
KEVIN'S VOICE. I'M PAYING FOR THIS HOUSE.
DORA'S VOICE. JUST PUSH IT.
KEVIN'S VOICE. I CAN HANDLE THIS DOOR. GET AWAY FROM ME. OW. *(The door crashes open, and Kevin stumbles in, followed by Dora. Lightning flashes. Thunder. Dora flicks on the light. The window is empty, except for the boom box, which is still playing.)*
KEVIN. You're going to pay for that session, Dora.
DORA. I'm not paying for that session.
KEVIN. Yes you are. The WHOLE session. *(Kevin goes up to the window, and turns off the boom-box.)*
DORA. Turn that back on. TURN IT ON. I DIDN'T GIVE YOU PERMISSION TO TURN THAT OFF.
KEVIN. I'M SPEAKING TO YOU AND I DON'T HAVE TO

* See Special Note on Songs and Recordings on copyright page.

31

ASK FOR YOUR PERMISSION.

DORA.   Fine. Go ahead. SPEAK. *(They stand there, glaring at each other. Then she turns, picks up Bill's bowl and takes it to the refrigerator. She opens the refrigerator, pulls out a head of lettuce and starts to shred it.)*

KEVIN.   Okay this is good. We're fighting. We're airing our differences. We're experiencing each other's individuality.

DORA.   I'm not going back.

KEVIN.   We made an appointment, Dora.

DORA.   YOU made an appointment.

KEVIN.   Because you went out to the car.

DORA.   Because you insulted me.

KEVIN.   I WANT TO MAKE LOVE TO YOU.

DORA.   *(Pleased.)* ... Kevin, we're having an argument.

KEVIN.   Great. Fabulous. You know something? I'm a decent guy. I've got a wife and a kid and a job.

DORA.   What do you want me to say?

KEVIN.   Don't say anything. Every time you open your mouth it gets worse. You know what I'm going to do? I'm going to leave. I'm going to get my rear-end out of here.

DORA.   BILL? YOUR DINNER'S READY.

KEVIN.   What you're doing is WRONG.

DORA.   No it's not.

KEVIN.   No it's not. You know what's wrong? I'm wrong. I'm doing something wrong, I know it's wrong, and I'm not this kind of person. Well, yes I am. No I'm not and I can stop myself. *(He starts to leave. She yells at the bathroom.)*

DORA.   BILL IF YOU DON'T GET OUT HERE IN THE NEXT 3 SECONDS I'M GOING TO FLUSH YOUR FOOD DOWN THE DISPOSAL. ONE. TWO.

KEVIN.   Just remember, Dora. I tried. I tried to save us. Remember that, before you go telling the next guy I walked out on you.

DORA.   THREE. *(He walks out. She runs to the door.)* Don't leave me.

KEVIN'S VOICE.   Shhhhhhhhh. *(Pause. Kevin reappears on the other side.)*

DORA.   Come back inside.

KEVIN. I can't.

DORA. Yes you can.

KEVIN. I'm afraid.

DORA. Come in. Kevin. Come inside.

KEVIN. I'm afraid of you. I'm afraid of Bill. I'm even afraid of Mrs. Middle.

DORA. Come back in here. Nobody's going to hurt you. Come in here. Come in here. *(He comes inside, and hangs by the door.)*

KEVIN. I just want to be happy, Dora. That's what we both want, isn't it? We just want to be happy.

DORA. Shhhhh. *(She is kissing him.)*

KEVIN. Don't do that.

DORA. Shhhhh. Shhhhhh. *(She is unbuttoning his shirt, and kissing his nipples.)*

KEVIN. I have to go home.

DORA. Don't go home.

KEVIN. I have to.

DORA. Shhhhhhh.

KEVIN. Oh God. Oh God Dora, what's going to happen to us? *(Suddenly they start tearing off their clothes. They are kissing. They are kissing and trying to take off their clothes while they're kissing. He picks her up, and starts to carry her to the bedroom.)*

DORA. No. Please. Not the bedroom.

KEVIN. Just this once —

DORA. That's where Gerry and I —

KEVIN. It's all right. It's all right. The table. *(He is carrying her to the table, setting her on it.)*

DORA. But Duane —

KEVIN. We don't have to do the table.

DORA. We can't do the floor. Please not the floor.

KEVIN. We'll do the sofa. We've done the sofa. You like the sofa.

DORA. I like the sofa. *(He is carrying her to the sofa.)*

KEVIN. Don't worry. Everything's fine. We're just fine. Above all, Do Not Worry.

DORA. I'm not worried.

KEVIN. My zipper's stuck.

DORA. What's wrong with your zipper?
KEVIN. I can do it MYSELF — *(Suddenly lightning and thunder crash into the window. Kevin looks up to see Bill sitting on the ladder, wearing the raincoat, watching them.)* JESUS CHRIST.
DORA. What.
KEVIN. GODDAMMIT, DORA.
DORA. What did I do? What did I do?
KEVIN. BILL!! *(As Kevin runs out the door, pulling up his pants, lightning crashes again. Bill is standing up on the ladder now, putting his hands on the glass and peering at Dora.)*
DORA. BILL, GET OUT OF THERE!
KEVIN'S VOICE. I'M GOING TO KILL HIM!
DORA. KEVIN DON'T HURT HIM! KEVIN!
KEVIN'S VOICE. *(Simultaneously.)* BILLL! *(Dora runs out after Kevin. Lightning. Thunder. The rain pours down.)*

Scene 12

Dawn. The rain has subsided, but the sky is an unrelenting gray. The swan has mud on his coat, and mud on his pants. He is sitting at the table with a black eye. Dora is applying iodine to it.

DORA. Franklin always said, he used to say, Dora if you can't love yourself, then you can't love anyone. I said, But Franklin — I love YOU.... Franklin was much too delicate for someone of my affections. If he hadn't left, I probably would have destroyed him altogether.

I don't think men are born on this planet. I think men are born on the planet Pluto and they have them molecularly disassembled and radared to the earth. Which is why. Which is why they are so, so, you have to take care of them in a very special way because they are foreign bodies being introduced to the system. And which is both why why I love them and why I don't understand them whatever they're talking about.

I remember I met Gerry, you would think it was the day after he'd been radared to the earth. There was something about Gerry. Something tender, something baby, like here was a man who needed more time to adapt to the eco-system. Gerry was always talking to himself, What is love and why do we do it? The day after we got married he went out in the woods and shot himself. The whole thing didn't exactly inspire my confidence.

Duane inspired my confidence, or what was left of it. Duane breathed life into a millimeter of myself, the piece of shrapnel I have come to regard as my heart. I took one look at Duane and said, Here's a man he doesn't ask questions, and he doesn't own a gun. Perfect, I thought, how could I go wrong? So I told him I loved him, and I loved myself. Duane said, How can you love yourself, if you don't love the world? Love the world, I said? I can hardly get out of bed. *(Then.)*

Two days later, he ran off. I was joking. *(She has gone to the refrigerator, gotten a piece of ice out of the freezer, and put it on the swan's eye, covering it with the swan's hand. He takes the ice off his eye, and licks it.)*

SWAN.   Mmmmbug. Mmmmbug.... Dirt. Mmmdirt. Mmmmbird. Mmmmmbird.

DORA.   Keep it on, don't take it off.

SWAN.   I am a bird.

I am a man.

I am a man.

DORA.   No, Bill.

SWAN.   I am a bird.

I am a bird.

I am a man.

DORA.   All right, fine. I'm going to go take a shower. *(He follows her.)*

SWAN.   I am a woman. I am a woman.

DORA.   No, Bill. You're a man. *(Beat.)* Forget it. It's five o'clock in the morning. We're both confused. *(She tries to exit, but he ducks in front of her, and gets in her way.)*

SWAN.   Dora is a bird.

DORA.   No. Dora is a woman.

SWAN.   Dora is a bird.

DORA.   No.

SWAN.   Dora is a bird. Dora is a bird — *(She slaps him on the nose, hard.)*

DORA.   STOP IT. STOP IT. JUST STOP IT. *(He hisses and barks at her. She hisses and barks back, and slaps him on the nose again.)* A person does not go through other people's garbage, A person does not hiss at other people, bite other people, jump down at them from the refrigerator, and most of all, most of all, a person does not stare at other people when they are having sex. *(She stops. They stare at each other.)*

SWAN.   I have a bell. *(Pause.)*

DORA.   No, Bill. *(She starts to go off. Again, he stops her.)*

SWAN.   There was a time like a forest. I had a bell in the forest. One day the bell came to the forest and said, Hold me. *(They stare at each other.)*

DORA.   Hold me?

SWAN.   Free me.

DORA.   Free you?

SWAN.   Like a rope like a chain Like a chain Like a vine Like a man Like an icicle —

DORA.   Don't. *(He is grabbing her by the wrist, and slowly forcing her to the floor beneath him.)*

SWAN.   Stars blood Everywhere there was blood —

DORA.   Bill —

SWAN.   Distances traveled to come — you —

DORA.   Don't hurt me — *(She struggles. He grabs her by the throat. He rattles at her like a gun.)*

SWAN.   Heart Heart Heart Heart Heart Heart —

DORA.   Bill. Don't. Let go. Let GO. *(She frees herself, and stumbles out of the house. He chases after her, but she is gone — the sound of her car screaming out of the driveway, nearly colliding with another car. Horns. Alone, the swan hurls himself into the darkest corner of the house, chewing on his skin.)*

SWAN.   Bug.... Dirt ... mmmmmmm Dirt mmmmmmmmmm Dirt mmmmmmmmmm Dirt. Her lips were two eyes.

Scene 13

Later. The sun is setting on the other side of the house. The swan is still sitting in the corner. He is making a weird, gnawing sound in the back of his throat. Darkness is growing around him.

After a moment, the door opens and Kevin enters with a cage of milk, and something in a paper bag. He puts the milk in the refrigerator, and pulls a piece of steak out of the bag. It is wrapped in plastic. He unwraps the plastic, and puts the steak on a plate.

KEVIN.   Hey, Bill. Bill. Look what I brought you ... Dora around? *(Kevin goes over and stands in front of the swan with the steak.)* Sorry about the other night. I didn't mean to hit you that hard. Well actually, I did. *(Still nothing.)* Filet mignon. Eight dollars a pound. *(He sets the plate on the floor, and pushes it with his foot until it stops next to the swan.)* This is what you call corn-fed. Can't get a steak like this anywhere else in the country. People die for a steak like this.
SWAN.   Steak.
KEVIN.   This steak is a hundred per cent. Hundred and ten. This steak is so good, they call it a TEACHER. *(Outside, the truck honks. Kevin yells.)* BE RIGHT THERE. *(Pause. To the swan.)* We'll go for a drive sometime. You and me. I'll show you the truck. Nice truck. Refrigeration unit. I keep 100 gallons of milk cold for up to 24 hours.
SWAN.   Fabulous.
KEVIN.   We'll go hunting together. Take a day. Take a weekend. Nice woods around here. Nice trees. Dark. Very dark. I'll make you wear a nice, bright color. *(He starts out again, then turns back once more.)* Tell Dora: Don't fry the steak, broil it. Please God. *(He exits. The truck roars off. The swan examines the steak, then pushes it away.)*

Scene 14

Night. No moon. The house is completely dark. There is a noise in the corner like a wasp. Suddenly, it falls silent.

A car quietly crunches into the driveway. A car door shuts. Dora approaches the other side of the screen door, and peers inside.

Silence.

She starts to pull open the screen door. It doesn't open. She pulls harder. It's locked.

DORA'S VOICE. *(Quietly.)* Bill?... Open the door. Open the door. *(Then.)* Bill. *Bill. (She pulls on the door again. She goes away. After a moment, the sound of someone grunting and straining in the bedroom. The light of a flashlight. The sound of a window, shutting. Something falls off a bureau. A figure appears in the doorway. It is Dora. Her hand feels for the switch, and she turns on the light. The swan is still in the corner. He moves further into the corner.)*

DORA. Hello, Bill.

SWAN. *Don't look at me. (Pause.)*

DORA. It's all right, Bill.

SWAN. *Don't look at me.*

DORA. I'm not looking at you.

SWAN. Don't come near me.

DORA. I'm not coming near you. *(Long pause.)* Maybe I'll just sit on the corner of the — *(As she starts toward him to sit down, he shrieks, lunging at her, striking out with his hands, missing. She scrambles back to the her side of the room, and he shrinks further into the corner, tearing at his clothes, his hair.)*

SWAN. Don't let me hurt you Don't let me hurt you Don't let me hurt you.

DORA. *(Simultaneously.)* Don't touch me goddammit DON'T TOUCH ME. *(Pause.)* I won't let you hurt me. *(He shudders*

38

heavily, then gives a giant twitch.)
SWAN. Evanesced.
DORA. Bill?
SWAN. Yes I thought love is the only thing that matters if I only could get me some I could laugh again I could eat again I could belong to the world —

Yukon Radio This is Yukon Radio Yukon Count on Us —

Mmmmmgbug Snow I kept Snow heading south but the ssssnow sssssnow kept getting deeper and the wind killing wind —

Centuries I was centuries to get as far as Kitimat and the sssnow ssssssnow was so big It was so big I was up to my eye eye eye So I decided to go inland but Inland it was deeper It was even so deep I dig Dug Crawled Snap Evanesced all the way to Prince George Jasper Red Deer Medicine Hat Hat Hat Hat —

Somewhere in the universe it stopped snowing for no reason no way no how the glass righted itself and the snow stopped spilling —

I dug a window. I broke a tunnel. I ate the sky. I ate the sky. And all around me was a vast white field ... the vast white field of God. And far away in the vast white field of lovelessness ... lovelessness ... I saw a figure, burrowing. Her name was Dora and her heart was a furnace of gold — *(He breaks off. His chest is heaving. His hands are opening and closing on air. She goes over to him, and stops several feet away.)*
DORA. Ssshhhh Sssshhhh —
SWAN. Ssshhhh Sssshhhh —
DORA. It's okay Bill I'm back —
SWAN. It's okay Bill I'm back —
DORA. I'm not going anywhere Everything's going to be all right —
SWAN. I'm not going anywhere Everything's going to be all right —
DORA. Shhhhhhhh
SWAN. Shhhhhhhh — *(Pause.)* Hold me — *(He reaches out. She backs away.)* Hold me — *(He reaches out. She backs away.)* Hold me — *(He reaches out. She backs away.)* Hold me — *(He*

reaches out. This time, she stands her ground. He gets closer and closer. He takes her hand and holds it to his cheek, like a little bird. To her hand.) Like a vine like a chain like a man like an icicle like an icicle — *(He is curling up around her hand, following it to her lap, and nestling inside it. He gets comfortable. Then.)* Tie. *(In the distance, an enormous truck roars down the highway. Far away, a dog erupts and starts barking. The dog keeps barking as long as it can, then finally gives up.)*

Scene 15

Darkness. The moon rises. It is blood-red. Dora is asleep on the sofa. The screen-door is banging gently against the frame. The swan is gone.

Dora opens her eyes. She stares at the steak on the floor. After a moment, she gets up and puts it in the refrigerator.

She pauses in front of the refrigerator, examining its contents. She reaches inside, and pulls out a piece of pizza.

She is chewing on the pizza, when a man comes out of the bathroom. He saunters over to her. The brim of a hat is pulled down over his face.

It is the swan. He is wearing a gorgeous suit, with a gorgeous fedora.

She finishes chewing, before she speaks.

DORA.   What's that?
SWAN.   What?
DORA.   That suit.
SWAN.   What?

DORA. Don't tell me what, tell me where you got it. Bill.
(Pause.)
SWAN. In the window.
DORA. You did not get it in the window. And it's not Franklin's, either. Bill? You didn't go downtown, did you? Bill? *(He is gently taking the pizza from her.)* Don't. *(He takes the pizza and puts it back in the refrigerator. Then he takes hold of her chin with his mouth.)*
SWAN. Nut. *(He puts his mouth on her cheek.)* Sky. *(He puts his mouth on her ear.)* Bell. *(He puts his mouth on her hair.)* Grass. *(He puts his mouth on her shoulder.)* Leg. *(He puts her fingers in his mouth.)* Foot.
DORA. Bill, I think you'd better get back in your basket. Bill. *(He sweeps her into his arms, like Fred Astaire.)*
SWAN. Cara mia.
DORA. Oh, my God. Italian. *(He sweeps her into a dip, takes off his hat and throws it away. They begin to dance. It's a tango. He directs her across the floor, then stops — bending her into another dip. He dives onto her fingers, kissing them, his lips wandering up the back of her hand onto her arm.)*
This is a dream. *(His lips are wandering up her neck. She pushes him away.)*
No. *(He directs her back across the floor in the opposite direction. Again, he stops, and bends her into a dip. This time, he dives onto her throat. She succumbs for a moment, then pushes him away.)*
Don't. *(He is directing her back across the room. At the other side, he pushes her into a twirl, and catches her.)*
Oh Bill. *(He grabs her by the hair, pulls her head back, and is about to kiss the living daylights out of her when suddenly, there is a rush of wind. The big wooden door blows open: moonlight. Dora turns.)*
Who's that? *(It's Kevin. His shadow stretches from the door, across the floor, and up the opposite wall, where the eye in its head burns like a comet. In its hand is a long knife. As the knife raises itself, and then stabs the air.)*
KEVIN KEVIN DON'T DO IT DON'T DO IT. *(Bells clang. Blackout.)*

Scene 16

Early morning. The swan is gone. Dora is sleeping on the sofa. Kevin stands over her, a cage of milk in one hand.

KEVIN. Did you sleep with him? *(Dora opens her eyes.)*

DORA. Why, Kevin. Hello.

KEVIN. It's five o'clock.

DORA. My pocketbook is on the counter.

KEVIN. Dora, we have a problem.

DORA. What day is it? *(She sits up.)*

KEVIN. Carol got the MasterCard bill.

DORA. Carol?

KEVIN. My wife.

DORA. I know who Carol is.

KEVIN. I mean she's furious. She's absolutely livid.

DORA. God, it's cold out. Isn't it cold out. I'm freezing.

KEVIN. Dora, you have got to stop charging everything.

DORA. I'm paying you back. I'm paying you back every penny of it.

KEVIN. You don't understand Carol. She likes to have everything paid up by the end of the month. She hates to pay interest. She won't. She won't. She just refuses. She refuses to pay interest.

DORA. All right, I heard you. God, it's cold. It's much too cold for July. July is not supposed to be this cold.

KEVIN. IT'S DECEMBER 16TH. *(She stares at him for several moments before she speaks.)*

DORA. It is?

KEVIN. I wouldn't bring it up, otherwise. If it was up to me, you could charge everything. *(She struggles out of bed, and her legs buckle beneath her. Kevin helps her up.)* Dora, are you all right?

DORA. Why am I so cold? I don't know why I'm so cold.

KEVIN. Well put some clothes on. *(As she heads for the bathroom, the swan emerges. His black eye is gone. He goes to the refrigerator, opens it, and stares into it. Dora watches him a moment, then*

42

hurries off.) What's going on, here? Dora? Speak to me.
DORA'S VOICE. YES?
KEVIN. Did you sleep with him? *(He stares at the swan, who is drinking milk from the bottle. Dora emerges, putting on a robe.)*
DORA. Did I what?
KEVIN. I said did you feed him? I can feed him if you want, while you get dressed. Do you want me to feed him? *(He is already finding the bread, tearing it up into the bowl.)* It's going to snow. Linda is making a snow-bird. Snow-man. She's making a big one. Bill is the devil.
DORA. Kevin, you're hysterical.
KEVIN. You're right, Dora, I'm hysterical. It's because I, it's because I, it's because I'm not sleeping, Dora. I can't think the last time I got a decent night's sleep.
DORA. You don't have to apologize.
KEVIN. I'M NOT APOLOGIZING. *(He screams at her. His voice is a monster. She backs away from him. He flies over the bed, catching her.)* I want to apologize. I do. Dora, you've been good about it, you really have. You've been very good about it. Me and Carol. You've never asked me for a thing. Other than the money. And I appreciate it. I really do. And Dora. Dora, I'd like to say ...
DORA. ... What?
KEVIN. Excuse me?
DORA. You were going to say? *(He stops. They both turn, and look at the swan, who is closing his eyes and sinking onto the sofa, instantly asleep.)*
KEVIN. Would you marry me?
DORA. ... Would I what?
KEVIN. Would you marry me, Dora?
DORA. ... Kevin, you ARE married.
KEVIN. I wanted to ask you the day I met you, but it was too late, I WAS ALREADY MARRIED. Would you marry me, Dora?
DORA. Oh Kevin. Why do you have to ask me NOW? Why didn't you ask me two years ago?
KEVIN. I should have asked you two years ago WHY DIDN'T I ASK YOU I was married you KNOW I was married I was

43

MARRIED. I should have divorced her the day I met you, I can get a divorce, I can still get a divorce, I'll get a divorce if you say the word, Dora. Say the word.

DORA. I — I — I — I don't know, Kevin, I —

KEVIN. I tried not to notice. I tried not to say anything when he came here, he's a swan I said, he's a wounded swan and it's not her fault she cares for him, she cares for everything, so what if it walks, it talks. My God, Dora, it talks! The animal stood up on its hind legs and talked to me, to you, and STILL I STOOD HERE, I STOOD HERE ON MY HIND LEGS AND SAID THAT'S OKAY, GIVE THE WOMAN HER PRIVACY WHY DON'T YOU??

DORA. Oh, Kevin.

KEVIN. So I did, I gave you your privacy, I sat in my house and made Carol dinner, I made Carol bookshelves, I took Carol dancing, I sanded the floor and painted the doghouse, I dreamed of you coming, holding me, holding me in your arms and kissing me, kissing me, your tongue, your tongue, I dreamed of you loving me till I cried like a baby.

DORA. Kevin, you know I can't marry you.

KEVIN. *(Overriding.)* You love me. You know you love me. You love me. You love me. *(Pause.)* You don't love me.

DORA. Yes I do. I DO.

KEVIN. Then why can't you marry me?

DORA. Kevin, I think we should have this discussion in front of George Cover.

KEVIN. We can't have this discussion in front of George Cover, we don't even have an APPOINTMENT.

DORA. All right, then, Kevin. Say we do want to get married. Say you propose to me, and I say yes.

KEVIN. I ALREADY PROPOSED.

DORA. That's right, you did. Now that you've proposed, what if I say yes? What if I do want to marry you, what are you going to do, then? Are you going to leave Carol? What about Linda?

KEVIN. Is that a yes?

DORA. Well it's kind of a yes and it's kind of a no. This is a very complicated issue and here's another thing: I'm still

44

married to Duane, at least technically. In a technical sense I am. I'd have to get a divorce from Duane before I could marry you. But what if Duane comes back? *(Pause.)*

KEVIN. This is a joke. *(He goes to the door.)*

DORA. No, Kevin, it's not a joke. It's a very complicated issue.

KEVIN. This is funny. This is hilarious.

DORA. Don't walk out while I'm talking to you, Kevin.

KEVIN. Milk. Pizza. Charge accounts. What was I thinking??

DORA. Kevin. Kevin.

KEVIN. What am I, some kind of jerk? *(He is out the door. Dora runs after him.)*

DORA'S VOICE. KEVIN! *(The truck roars out of the driveway. From the sofa, the swan opens his eyes a crack, and watches the screen-door fall gently closed. He closes his eyes again Pause. Pause. Dora comes back in. She looks at him, hard. Then she goes to the phone, and dials.)*

DORA. I'd like to leave a message for Kevin. This is Dora Hand. Dora. He'll be there in about five minutes. Would you tell him he left something here, and he has to come back and get it? He has to come back right away. It's very important. Thank you. *(She hangs up. The swan opens his eyes a crack, and watches her, as she dials again.)* I'd like to leave a message for Kevin. He's going to arrive there in about ten minutes. This is Dora. Dora Hand. Would you tell him to come back, right away? He left something important. It's VERY important. *(She hangs up, and looks at the swan. She goes off. The sound of drawers shutting and closing. Pause. She enters with a suitcase, which she sets beside the kitchen door. She goes over to the swan, and gives him a push.)* Yes, thank you, I'm freezing. It's freezing in here, the day's half over, and and it's upsetting, Bill. I'm upset. And, and, and, and I've decided I've been thinking about it, and I want you to leave ... Bill.

SWAN. Dora.

DORA. It's not because of you. Well of course it's because of you, but it's not your fault. I mean, Bill — you're a — you're a — you're a — Look at you. Look at me. Bill.

SWAN. Dora.

DORA.   I've packed a suitcase for you. It's got some clothes, and a change of underwear. In my experience, it's better to do it fast, so hurry up. BILL. *(She opens the screen door, propping it with a chair.)*
SWAN.   Dora.
DORA.   Please don't say anything, please please don't say anything. Just get up. Get up and get your coat on.
SWAN.   No.
DORA.   All right, then don't get your coat on. Just go. GO. *(She comes over, grabs him by the wrist, and drags him off the sofa. He clings to her.)*
SWAN.   No.
DORA.   Come on. Come ON. *(She is hauling him across the floor. He grabs onto a chair. She pries him away from it.)*
SWAN.   No.
DORA.   Come ON. *(He comes free of the chair and hurtles across the floor, grabbing onto the counter, the table, anything.)*
SWAN.   Dora.
DORA.   Let go.... Let. GO. *(She pries his fingers away from the counter, and he falls on the floor.)*
SWAN.   Ow.
DORA.   I'm sorry I'm sorry but you've got to — *(He grabs onto her.)*
SWAN.   Love me —
DORA.   NO —
SWAN.   Love me —
DORA.   NO — *(She's pushed him as far as the door, but he won't go through. He braces himself against the door-frame, as she pushes with all her might.)*
SWAN.   I'm caught in my body I'm deep in my body underground I'm miles beneath the surface if only you'd love me —
DORA.   GO. GO. GO.
SWAN.   *(Overriding.)* Bell Nut Sky The ground —
DORA.   GO — *(She pushes him out, but he comes back in. She tries to kick him away, but he hangs onto her knees. She tries to crawl away, but he crawls after her, reaching her, climbing her body, hand over hand, like Mount Everest.)*
SWAN.   The ground softens, flowers begin to to to breathe,

horses open their eyes, trees, forests, whole whole whole
COUNTRIES STRETCH THEIR MOUTHS AND LOVE ME
they say HOLD ME they say I AM CAUGHT IN MY BODY I
AM A PRISONER OF MY SOUL BUT YOUR LOVE WILL SET
ME FREE AND I WANT TO BE FREE I WANT SO MUCH TO
BE FREE I WILL DO ANYTHING IT TAKES ANYTHING IT
TAKES ANYTHING — *(He is holding her, holding her whole body
until she finally stops kicking, and stops crawling. She lies there, ex-
hausted.)* I can't go back. *(Pause. She turns around, and looks at
him. Pause. She kisses him. He shudders heavily. She kisses him again.
He shudders again, and then rolls over her. They begin to make love.
The sky grows dark. The walls disappear and the moon comes out.
Music from a radio. The lights of community, burning. The voices of
children, playing — they scream with terror and delight.)*

Scene 17

*The darkness fades. Morning appears. Dora lies on the floor,
sleeping. She is alone. The phone rings. It rings several times
before she picks it up.*

DORA.   Hello? *(No one. She hangs up. She gets up, and reaches
for her bathrobe.)* Bill? *(She goes off, looking for him.)*
DORA'S VOICE.   BILL? *(She reappears. She hurries to the win-
dow and looks out.)*
DORA.   Bill? *(She crosses to the kitchen.)* BILL? *(She starts to run
out the door.)* BILLLLL! *(She stops, as Kevin limps in. He is caked
with mud up to his knees, has a big black eye, and is carrying a wed-
ding dress.)*
KEVIN.   Hello.
DORA.   What are you doing here? What do you want?
KEVIN.   Put this on. Don't ask any questions, just put it on.
We're leaving town. *(He throws the wedding dress on the table. She
is finding the rifle.)*
DORA.   Did you get my message?
KEVIN.   About five times.

47

DORA. Did you get my message?

KEVIN. I said yes. What are you doing with the gun?

DORA. Don't move.

KEVIN. What are you doing?

DORA. Bill is gone.

KEVIN. What do you mean? *(She raises the rifle, and points it at him.)* Jesus.

DORA. You tell ME.

KEVIN. What are you talking about? I didn't do anything.

DORA. WHERE DID HE GO?

KEVIN. I DIDN'T DO ANYTHING.

DORA. KEVIN.

KEVIN. FOR JESUS' SAKE, DORA, I CAN'T THINK WHEN YOU'RE POINTING THAT THING AT ME. PUT THE GUN DOWN. PUT THE GUN DOWN.

DORA. Okay fine. This isn't getting us anywhere. *(She lowers the rifle.)*

KEVIN. Thank you. May I speak now? *(This is it.)* I'm leaving Carol. I'm getting out of here. They can accuse me of theft, larceny, I don't care. We've got the entire map of the United States laid out before us, Dora. COME LIVE WITH ME AND BE MY LOVE. *(She raises her rifle. He backs away, reaching for the table, a spoon, a cup, anything in self-defense.)*

DORA. What's the matter with your eye?

KEVIN. What do you mean?

DORA. That's a black eye, where did you get it?

KEVIN. What do you mean where did I get it — *(He crashes into a chair, and sits down.)*

DORA. STAND UP. *(He struggles to his feet.)*

KEVIN. I'M STANDING UP.

DORA. DID YOU KILL HIM?

KEVIN. HOW COULD YOU SAY SUCH A THING —

DORA. YOU KILLED HIM, DIDN'T YOU?

KEVIN. NO OF COURSE NOT —

DORA. WHAT DID YOU DO GODDAMMIT — *(She stops. She is working the rifle.)*

KEVIN. What? What's the matter?

DORA. The safety. The safety's stuck.

KEVIN. Don't cry.

DORA. I'M NOT CRYING.

KEVIN. Well don't get excited, you'll accidentally fire it — *(He starts toward her. She raises the rifle again.)*

DORA. I fixed it.

KEVIN. DON'T POINT IT, DORA. GODDAMN YOU. GODDAMN YOU, I DIDN'T DO ANYTHING TO HIM, HE'S LEFT, CAN'T YOU SEE THAT? HE'S LEFT, HE'S GONE. THE SON OF A BITCH HAS LEFT YOU, GET IT? *(She stares at him. The rifle begins to shake.)* Now put down the gun. Put down the gun. *(The rifle is lowered. It is shaking even more. It goes on the sofa-bed.)* Thank you. We can be rational. We can be two adults. Not on the bed. Under the bed. Put it under the bed. Way under. *(It goes under the bed. He takes it out, and holds onto it.)*

DORA. He didn't leave me.

KEVIN. Of course he left you. Why shouldn't he? Everybody else has.

DORA. He didn't leave me. He loved me.

KEVIN. Big deal. Franklin loved you. Gerry loved you. Duane loved you.

DORA. But don't you understand, I could have loved him *back. (Pause.)*

KEVIN. You don't mean that.

DORA. I do. I do. Now he's gone. My big chance. He was my big chance.

KEVIN. There's no such thing as a big chance.

DORA. Yes there is. There is. *(Pause.)*

KEVIN. Okay okay. But Dora honey. Dora, I could be your big chance too. You can find a maniac any day of the week. You can do the maniacs, Dora, or you can do ME. Do ME. Choose ME. Somebody who can love you, who can protect you and take care of you, and give you things. Whatever you want. I can give you a house and a garden and a pool too if that's what you want. I can get it for you. I can. I will. Whatever you want. *(She is quiet for a long time. When she speaks, it is almost inaudible.)* I can't hear you.

DORA. I said, Get me out of here. *(Pause.)* Get me OUT. I WANT OUT.

KEVIN. That's right. That's right, Dora. Fuck them. Fuck all of them. I've got to find another truck. Put on that dress. I'll be back as soon as I can. *(He runs out the door. He runs back in.)* We Refuse to Spend the Rest of Our Lives Being Unhappy. We Absolutely and Categorically Refuse. *(He runs out.)*

Scene 18

Night. Dora alone. She is holding the white dress.

DORA. And that was how it started. I wanted you to touch me, and so I made you. The ice cracked. Like thunder, like an earthquake, the ice separated under my feet and

Help me, Hold me, I'm caught in my body, I'm dying inside my body but your love could set me free and I want so much to be free

Somewhere in another country a field of white a valley of lovelessness ... I turned and felt the weight of you, your ribs and your struggle, the pressure of your heart racing, my ears pounding and your breath fell in my ear all wet like a fog, and too late for second thoughts because we were running, we were running together as fast as we could and suddenly your wings busted through the ice, the glacier tumbled and separated from the land, the water broke beneath us and forget the water you were with me you held me in your arms you held me and and and

What is love? Why do we do it? *It defies the law of gravity.*

The next thing I remember there was no sound anywhere, nowhere in the world was there a sound except for the spinning-sound, like the whirring of the universe the moment you grabbed me, and you fixed your terrible eye on me, it was like a hammer. *(She picks up the dress, puts it on over her head, and pulls it down.)*

Scene 19

Night. Outside, it is snowing. Dora is in the wedding dress, frantically dragging a suitcase out of the bedroom. It is enormously heavy.

She goes off again, and is returning with another suitcase, equally heavy, as a truck pulls into the driveway, and a door slams.

KEVIN'S VOICE.   DORA I'M BACK. YOU READY? *(Kevin throws open the door. The bruise stands out on his cheek like a plum. He is wearing a nice dark suit.)*
KEVIN.   Does it fit? *(She throws him a rope, and hurries off to the bedroom.)*
DORA.   Hurry.
KEVIN.   What's the rope for?
DORA'S VOICE.   Tie up the suitcases.
KEVIN.   We don't have to tie them up, we can just throw them in the back of the, the, the — *(As she returns with another suitcase, she collapses.)* Dora honey, are you all right?
DORA.   Leave me alone. Leave me alone. Just get the flashlight.
KEVIN.   I'll get the flashlight. Dora, you're cold.
DORA.   I'm cold. I'm cold, that's why, that's why we've got to get out of here, we've got to run away.
KEVIN.   Okay.
DORA.   We refuse to be unhappy. We absolutely and categorically refuse to be unhappy.
KEVIN.   Put on a coat. Where's your coat?
DORA.   Find the flashlight. FIND THE FLASHLIGHT.
KEVIN.   I'll find the flashlight if you'll put on a that's the ax. What are you doing with the ax? *(She is dragging the ax out from under the bed.)*
DORA.   We can't leave the house without an ax.
KEVIN.   Dora, we're ELOPING. *(She stops, suddenly. She stares*

at the ax in her hands, and then suddenly puts it down.)
DORA. You're right. We'll take the gun. The gun's much better.
KEVIN. Don't scare me. You're scaring me, Dora.
DORA. Kevin don't argue with me. What did you do with the gun?
KEVIN. We can't elope like this. I REFUSE TO ELOPE LIKE THIS.
DORA. KEVIN LISTEN TO ME IT'S SNOWING OUT THERE.
KEVIN. Yeah, so? *(She reaches out with one long arm, grabs him by the collar, and pulls him close.)*
DORA. Bill is coming back.
KEVIN. This is a good suit. *(Her strength is tremendous. She holds him fast.)*
DORA. Bill is coming back. Now MOVE. *(She releases him, and starts pulling the cushions off the sofa.)*
KEVIN. Bill isn't coming back.
DORA. What did you do with the gun? Oh God he lost the gun. He lost the gun.
KEVIN. *He's not coming back. (She looks up: light-bulb.)*
DORA. Florida. We'll go to Florida. Florida's two thousand miles from here. He'll never find us in Florida. *(Suddenly her legs give way again.)*
KEVIN. Dora, what's the matter with your legs?
DORA. Heart heart heart heart heart heart — *(He is running to the refrigerator, pouring a glass of milk.)*
KEVIN. You've caught a cold, that's what. You caught a cold because you've been walking around in your bathrobe which is because you're alone too much, I keep telling you, it's not healthy to be alone so much.
DORA. Bill is coming back. Bill is coming back. Bill is coming back. *(He is running to Dora, pushing the glass of milk at her.)*
KEVIN. Drink some milk.
DORA. I'm not thirsty.
KEVIN. DRINK SOME MILK. EVERYBODY UNDERESTIMATES THE POWER OF MILK. *(She starts to drink it, then stops. She looks up, terrified.)*

52

DORA. He's here. He's here.

KEVIN. What? Bill? *(She runs to the door, and shuts it, locks it.)*

DORA. QUICK.

KEVIN. He's not out there. *(She stares at Kevin for a moment. For a moment, she turns away and starts chewing on her skin. Then, with a great effort, she pulls herself out of it.)*

DORA. Kevin. Kevin. I always loved you. You've got to know I always loved you.

KEVIN. What's that? What are you doing?

DORA. Tell me you love me. Tell me you love me RIGHT NOW.

KEVIN. But it's Christmas. The choir is beautiful. The pageant is gorgeous.

DORA. TELL ME YOU LOVE ME.

KEVIN. ... I love you. *(She grabs him, and holds onto him like a life-raft.)*

DORA. Bell. Nut. Sky. Sky.

KEVIN. This isn't happening. This isn't happening.

DORA. There was a time like a forest. There was a time like a forest.

KEVIN. Stop it. Stop it, Dora. He's not out there. I got rid of him. I took him away, I had to. He's miles away from here. Miles. I'm sorry honey but I love you so much, I love you, I love you — *(He is kissing her on the face, the mouth. Suddenly he stops.)* What's wrong with your mouth?

DORA. My mouth?

KEVIN. Your mouth is bleeding. WHY IS YOUR MOUTH BLEEDING?? *(Dora touches her mouth. A bright dot of blood.)*

DORA. My mouth? *(He runs for the phone. She starts for the window.)*

KEVIN. It's all right, Dora. It's all right. I'm going to call the police. I'm going to call the police and get them over here.... The phone doesn't work.

DORA. The phone?

KEVIN. I gave you a check, what did you do with the check?

DORA. The check?

KEVIN. Oh God, we're in so much trouble. I'm going out to the truck. DON'T FOLLOW ME. I'm going out to the truck, and call the police. I'll be right back. You hear me, Dora?

DORA. Am I going someplace?

KEVIN. You're right here, Dora.

DORA. Oh God. I am, aren't I? BILLLLL — *(She runs to the window. A plane approaches, overhead.)*

KEVIN. That's not Bill. That's a plane. *(She puts her lips to the glass, and whispers something to it.)* ... I love you, Dora Hand. *(He runs out. Like magic, the great wooden door closes itself. She turns and looks out the window. Bill arrives. He is wearing the trench coat. He has been running. He has been running for miles. His coat is covered with mud, there is mud on his face, and leaves in his hair. He reaches out to her.)*

DORA. Bill. *(Kevin is back at the door, rattling the doorknob.)*

KEVIN'S VOICE. DORA, THE DOOR'S LOCKED! OPEN THE DOOR! OPEN THE DOOR! *(Dora runs to the window.)* DORA, IT'S LOCKED! COME AWAY AND OPEN THE DOOR! *(Dora is climbing into the window, her white dress catching the light like the moon, as she reaches out to Bill and he reaches out to her. Kevin is banging on the door.)* ALL RIGHT, DORA! IT'S GOING TO BE ALL RIGHT! I'M GOING TO BREAK IT DOWN! I'M GOING TO BREAK IT DOWN, DORA! GET AWAY FROM THE DOOR! I'M COMING IN! ONE! TWO! THREE! *(With a great crash, Kevin breaks down the door, and the lights go out. There is a huge noise: glass breaking, the world breaking, a tree cracking, Dora and Bill escaping, getting free, and last of all, wind, nothing but wind. Kevin stumbles to a lamp and turns it on. He looks at the window. There is an enormous hole in the middle of it. Snow is blowing in, from the window, from the door. Music: a plaintive Parisian melody — part tango, part blues.)*

THE END

PROPERTY LIST

Flashlight (DORA)
Rope (DORA)
Ax (DORA)
Rifle (DORA)
Bottles of milk (KEVIN)
Drinking glasses (KEVIN, DORA)
Box of pizza (KEVIN)
Hairbrush (DORA)
White nurse's dress (DORA)
Nurse's cap (DORA)
Purse (DORA)
Sweater (DORA)
Kitchen towel (DORA)
Gun (KEVIN)
Bowl (for milk) (DORA)
Blanket (DORA)
Pillow (DORA)
Tape, 2 rolls for window (KEVIN)
Boombox (DORA)
Cassette (DORA)
Vacuum cleaner (KEVIN)
Bag of groceries (DORA) with:
	head of lettuce
	box of sprouts
Dog bowl (DORA)
2 beer bottles (DORA)
Checkerboard with checkers (DORA)
Bag of chips (DORA)
Dead rabbit (KEVIN)
Cowboy jacket, distressed (DORA)
Small make-up mirror (DORA)
Bolo tie (SWAN)
Socks (SWAN)
Dead mouse (SWAN)
Iodine (DORA)

Ice (DORA)
Paperbag (KEVIN) with:
    milk
    steak
Plate (KEVIN)
Knife (KEVIN)
Bread (KEVIN)
Suitcases (DORA)
Wedding dress (KEVIN)

SOUND EFFECTS

Bump as something hits the window
Phone ring
Toilet flushes
Car door slam
Truck horn
Jumbo jet
Bath water running
Birds twittering
Breeze blowing
Thunder
Rain
Car pulling up
Car horn
Wasp buzzing
Car quietly pulling into driveway
Window shutting
Distant truck roar
Dogs barking
Music from radio
Children playing
Bells clanging
Truck roaring out of driveway
Glass breaking
Tree cracking
Wind

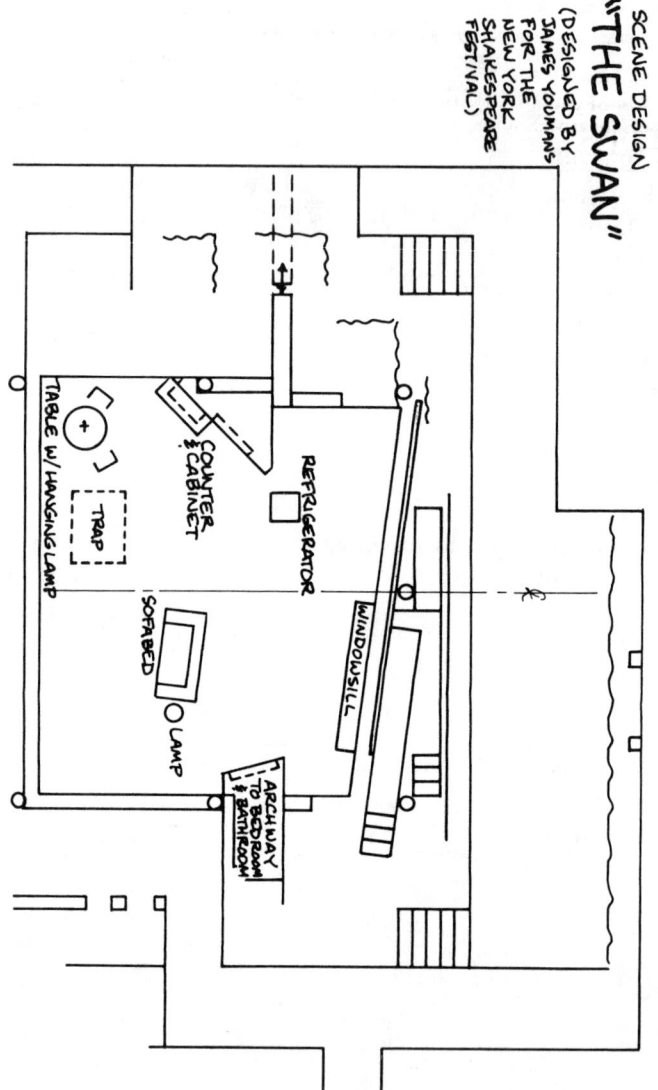

SCENE DESIGN
"THE SWAN"

(DESIGNED BY
JAMES YOUMANS
FOR THE
NEW YORK
SHAKESPEARE
FESTIVAL)

TABLE W/ HANGING LAMP

TRAP

COUNTER & CABINET

REFRIGERATOR

SOFABED

LAMP

WINDOWSILL

ARCHWAY TO BEDROOM & BATHROOM